Staining & Painting
FLOORS

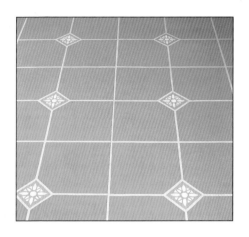

MICHAEL CLARK

MINI · WORKBOOK · SERIES

MURDOCH
B O O K S

CONTENTS

Stencilled floor (top left), crackle-effect floor (far left) and imitation granite tiles (left)

Decorating floors

Decorating a floor can be one of the most satisfying do-it-yourself tasks you will ever undertake. Just be sure that your chosen finish is durable enough to survive constant foot traffic, especially if it is in a living room or hallway.

Several coats of clear finish protect this imitation parquet floor. A matt or satin finish allows the decoration to be seen more clearly than would a gloss one.

PAINTED FLOORS
Painting a floor offers limitless scope for colour and design, and it is by far the most inexpensive method of making any floor look attractive, no matter what its condition. However, it can be time-consuming if you choose an intricate design.

Floors can be painted all over, given a colour wash or limewash, treated to achieve an aged, crackle effect, made to resemble stone paving or decorated with a design either by painting freehand or stencilling. Examples of these techniques are given in the book.

Correctly sealed for protection, painted floors are easily maintained and wear exceptionally well. They will change subtly as they age and are subjected to traffic, but this can be quite attractive. The secret is not to

Floors can be painted to produce a natural-looking result as here, or you can emphasize the painting by using shapes or colours that are not found in nature.

skimp on the clear protective coating. A solid protective finish, which may actually be two or three coats, will last for many years. An additional protective coat can be applied every year or two.

CLEAR FINISHES

There are a number of different coatings classed as clear finishes, including polyurethane finishes, oils and waxes. The desired look and the natural beauty of the floor will influence the overall finishing approach taken.

Applying a clear polyurethane or oil coating, or staining and then clear-coating, is obviously quicker than applying an elaborate painted finish. Waxing, however, will involve a lot more work.

STENCILS

The use of stencils is a decorative technique that can produce a stunning floor. The designs can be as simple or intricate as you choose. You can use paints in any colour combination to suit your room, or you can use stains over a clear finish.

There are a number of stencil projects in the book, demonstrating the variety of uses to which stencils can be put. They include painting designs over an already painted floor (pages 40 and 54) or a stained floor (page 30).

PREPARATION

As with any painting, careful preparation of the surface is the key to success. See pages 6–9 for timber floors and page 9 for concrete ones.

Preparing timber floors

Floors that will receive a clear coating require more preparation than those that will have a painted finish, but all will need some degree of sanding and filling to ensure a sound, durable finish.

TOOLS AND MATERIALS

- Claw hammer and nail punch
- Pliers
- Upright power sander★
- Hand sander
- Cork sanding block
- Abrasive paper
- Dusting brush

- Bleach and scrubbing brush (optional)
- Filling blades
- Filler knife
- Wood filler
- Clear sealer
- Protective glasses and dust mask

★ Can be hired

CLEANING UP
Before sanding the floor, carefully inspect the entire floor surface for any protruding nail heads or tacks. Also look for obvious splits on the edges of the floorboards. If you do not remove these hazards before you begin work, you could injure yourself or damage the sanding machine.

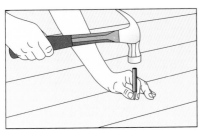

Hammer in any protruding nail heads and use a nail punch to drive them below the surface.

Nail down loose boards and knock in protruding nail heads with a nail punch and hammer. Remove any protruding objects with pliers or a claw hammer.

If the floor has an existing wax coating you will have to remove it before sanding, or the coating will clog the abrasive paper. Use a commercial wax stripper for the task, rinse the floor clean and allow it to dry. Always follow the instructions on the container.

If there is an existing opaque paint coating on the floor and you want to apply a clear finish, you will have to remove the paint. This can be achieved by three different methods: heat gun, liquid paint stripper or sanding. Whichever method you

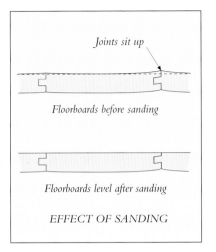

Joints sit up

Floorboards before sanding

Floorboards level after sanding

EFFECT OF SANDING

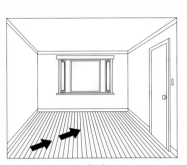

1 First sand diagonally from corner to corner.

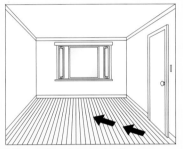

2 Repeat from the opposite direction.

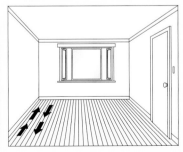

3 Change to fine abrasive paper and sand in the direction of the floorboards.

SANDING A FLOOR

choose, make sure there is good ventilation in the room. Deep sanding is the best way to remove a stained finish.

SANDING

Floorboards that are to receive a clear finish will need a thorough sanding to achieve the best result. If the floor has an existing clear finish and you are going to re-coat it, then a light sand is all that is needed. Clean away the dust and apply the new coat.

New timber boards will require a little more work before you can apply a clear coating. When new tongue-and-groove floorboards are laid, there can be a tendency for the joints to 'sit up' (see the diagram above) and you will need to make the floor smooth and level.

Use an upright power sanding machine to do the job. This will be much quicker than using a small electric hand sander. Upright machines can be hired, and the hire store will advise you how to operate them and fit the abrasive paper. They have dust-collection attachments, but dust will still escape. Be sure to wear a dust mask. Hand sanders are used for edges and corners. Do these with the appropriate abrasive paper after each stage with the upright sander. You may need to use a scraper for tight corners.

1 Remove the furniture from the room and seal doors into other parts of the house to contain the dust. Open all windows.

2 Fit coarse abrasive paper to the upright machine, switch it on and lower it gently to the floor. It will move forward and you should guide it at a steady pace. Always keep the machine moving on the surface so that it does not dig into the floorboards and leave unsightly scars. Sand the floor in a diagonal direction (from one corner to the other). When you reach the corner, tilt the machine and turn it. Overlap each strip slightly as you go (see the top diagram on page 7). Repeat the process in the opposite direction.

3 Change the paper to medium and sand in the direction of the boards, and then use fine paper. Vacuum up all the wood dust.

BLEACHING A FLOOR

If you want to lighten the colour of the sanded floor you can bleach it.

> **HINT**
>
> Inhaling timber dust may cause respiratory problems. Always wear a mask when sanding, especially when working with hardwoods such as teak or with chemically impregnated timber.

Ordinary domestic bleach, scrubbed in and rinsed off with clean water, will do a lot to lighten a floor. You can also purchase stronger chemical bleaches, which are applied in stages. These should be used in accordance with the manufacturer's instructions. Take care, as the concentrated fumes can be dangerous. Wear a protective mask and open all doors and windows to ensure good ventilation.

REPAIRING FAULTS

After sanding, fill any knot holes, cracks or nail holes. First apply a thin coat of clear or sanding sealer around the defect so that the dye or tint colour in the filling compound will not spread further than the hole or crack it was meant for. Then apply the stopping (filling) compound with a filler knife to obtain a firm, flat finish to the hole.

Take care when choosing the colour of the filler compound. Proprietary compounds come in a range of colours to match specific timber types. Timber has natural variations in colour, so it may be necessary to use several colours to disguise the surface imperfections.

Try out the filler first on a piece of matching floorboard.

Common filling materials are:

• Linseed oil filler. This soft filler takes a long time to harden. It is traditionally used for filling nail holes. The filler can be coloured to suit the natural timber or stain.

• Lacquer filler. This fast-drying filler dries hard and can be sanded level. Apply it to bare timber as the lacquer base can penetrate and discolour most stains. It comes in a variety of colours that can be mixed to obtain special colours.

• Water-based filler. This is a fast-drying material that dries hard and can be easily sanded. Use it on interior timbers before staining and finishing. It is ideal for repairing deep holes, although two or more applications may be required. It can be tinted to match the required finish. If you are going to stain the floor choose a lighter colour of filler, as it will become darker when the stain is applied.

Leave the filler to dry, then sand with abrasive paper around a cork block so the floor is flat and smooth.

PREPARING CONCRETE FLOORS FOR PAINTING

If concrete is new or 'green' it will contain some water. New concrete should be left for three to four weeks to allow all moisture to evaporate before you paint it.

An old concrete floor will need thorough cleaning. Use a high-pressure water blaster to remove all dirt and grime, and allow the surface to dry out completely before painting it. These pressure cleaners can be hired.

Previously painted concrete should also be high-pressure cleaned. If the surface has been finished with a gloss finish, you will need to provide a 'key' for the new base coat by giving the surface a good sand.

Always use paving or concrete paints, as they are designed for heavy foot traffic and for areas subject to weathering. They are non-slip, have a low sheen and come in a range of colours.

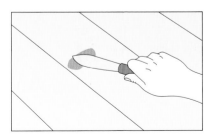

Seal any holes in the floorboards and then use a filler knife to apply a suitable filling compound.

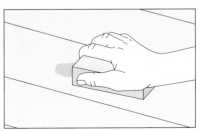

Once the filler is dry, use abrasive paper and a cork block to sand it back so that the floor is flat and smooth.

The tools used for decorating floors are not expensive and are readily available from most hardware stores. If they are looked after correctly, they can be reused a number of times.

Tools and techniques

The basic equipment and methods used to paint floors are the same as those used for any paint job. For the best result, always use the correct tools and techniques.

APPLICATION TOOLS

The tools most commonly used when applying decorative finishes to floors are paintbrushes and rollers.

PAINTBRUSHES

Although there are many types of brushes for particular tasks, the home decorator really needs only a few of them. They are known as flat brushes, and they come in a range of sizes. The most suitable ones for general use are 50 mm, 75 mm and 100 mm wide.

- The 50 mm brush is used to apply paint to small areas, for staining and for applying clear coatings.
- The 75 mm brush is used to apply paint to slightly larger areas, such as skirting boards, architraves or doors.
- The 100 mm brush is used for painting any large area, such as a wall, ceiling or floor.

When you are selecting a brush, don't consider price before quality. Cheap brushes tend to have plastic handles and short bristles that don't hold the paint well, thus making it harder to apply the paint. A good-quality brush has a strong hardwood handle, a copper- or nickel-plated steel stock and good-quality pure bristle or synthetic filling.

PAINT ROLLERS

There are a number of roller covers available. Each is specific for a task and type of paint. The right roller cover will give you an excellent finish, whereas the wrong cover will leave a finish that is disappointing.

- Lambswool covers are most commonly used for the application of matt emulsion paints. The most appropriate pile length for this purpose is 10 mm.
- Synthetic-fibre covers are used for applying emulsion gloss and semi-gloss paints. The pile length should be between 7 and 10 mm.
- Mohair covers are used to apply oil-based gloss and semi-gloss enamels. They are specifically designed for smooth surfaces such as walls and flush doors. These sleeves have a pile of 7 mm.
- Polyester sleeves are designed for use on rough to semi-rough surfaces. Most paints can be applied with these sleeves, with the exception of gloss enamel. The pile length is 20 mm.
- Foam rubber sleeves are used to apply gloss and semi-gloss enamels and clear finishes. To achieve a high-gloss finish on smooth surfaces, you may have to lay off the paint with a brush (see step 3, page 14 for laying

off) after using the roller. The pile length is 5–7 mm.

The width of roller sleeves ranges from 120 mm to 460 mm, with the most common being 225 mm. You will need a roller frame or cage of an appropriate width to slide the sleeve onto. Depending on the task, an extension pole may also be necessary. These are available in fixed sizes or as telescopic extension poles.

A roller tray is essential. These come in a range of sizes to cater for different roller widths and different quantities of paint. When you come to clean the roller, you will find it useful to have a wire loop that is designed to slip over the sleeve to squeeze out excess paint.

APPLYING PAINT BY BRUSH

The way a brush is held and the application technique used are the two most important factors for a satisfactory painting job.

The most common complaints from home decorators are physical fatigue and how messy painting can be. Both result from not holding the brush correctly and, following on from that, the way the paint is applied to the surface.

The brush is often gripped or held incorrectly. There are three ways of holding a paintbrush, and each has a specific purpose. There is a basic grip, the pencil grip and the overhead grip.
• Basic grip. Hold the brush between your thumb and first finger and apply pressure on the stock with the rest of your fingers (see the diagram opposite). This grip is perfect for painting flat, broad areas such as walls, flush doors and large areas of floors.
• Pencil grip. Hold the handle of the brush the same way as you would a pencil, between your thumb and first finger. This will give you a grip on the brush that is comfortable and perfect for cutting in or painting intricate detailed work.
• Overhead grip. By holding the brush with all your fingers around the handle and your thumb resting on top of the ferrule (metal band), you will achieve a comfortable grip for what can be tiring work, such as painting a ceiling.

LOADING THE BRUSH

Loading paint onto the brush is crucial in the application process. Too much paint and it goes everywhere, causing defects in the surface; too little paint and you have to work twice as hard and you may still produce defects.

Good-quality bristle – natural and synthetic – is tapered and has split ends (imagine the split ends of hair). These enable the bristles to hold the paint so that you achieve a fine finish free from brushmarks when you lay off correctly.

The following steps will allow you to load paint on a brush correctly.

1 Hold the brush firmly using the most comfortable grip (see the diagram on the opposite page).

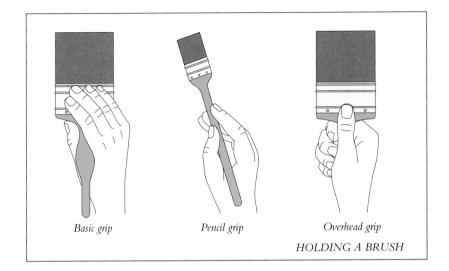

Basic grip *Pencil grip* *Overhead grip*

HOLDING A BRUSH

2 Dip the brush into the paint pot, no more than one-third the length of the bristle. Remember, this is the part that holds the paint.

3 Lift the bristles out of the paint and gently tap the inside of the pot with the tip of both sides of the brush. Three to four taps should do it. This will remove the excess paint from the bristles. Try always to tap the brush to the same side of the pot as this will leave a dry side that you can

lean the brush against when you stop for a break.

4 The brush is now loaded and ready for use.

Using this method you will be surprised how much paint the brush will hold, and without dripping. To prove the point, load the brush as explained, hold it above the paint pot and see how long it takes before the paint begins to drip.

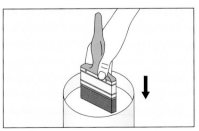

2 Dip the brush in the paint pot, inserting no more than one-third the length of the bristle.

3 Lift the bristles out of the paint and gently tap the inside of the pot with the tip of both sides of the brush.

Avoid painting from a new paint can as you cannot tap the bristles on the inner side to remove excess paint. Pour paint into another pot, filling it to one-third of its capacity.

After loading the brush several times, it may be necessary to wipe it on the lip of the pot to remove paint that has accumulated on the bristles. This will prevent paint running down the handle, which may happen if you tilt the brush upwards.

APPLYING THE PAINT

On horizontal surfaces such as floors, start at the point furthest away from you (or the door) and work your way across. If you are painting the floor of a whole room, ensure difficult areas such as behind doors are done before you paint your way out of the door. Always work over a manageable area: if you brush out over too large an extent you will have a disappointing, uneven finish.

There are a few basic steps that should be followed when applying the paint, so that you achieve an even finish with a minimum of brushmarks. These steps should be followed for each brush load applied.

1 Place the brush on the surface to be painted, keeping the brush at about 45 degrees to the surface. Use the full length of the bristle and move the brush horizontally across the area in a criss-cross fashion.

2 Once the paint is on the surface, spread it out evenly, maintaining an even pressure on the brush.

3 Remove any excess paint from the brush by scraping the bristles on one side of the pot. Using only the tips of the bristles and a minimum of pressure, gently lay off (work over) the paint to eliminate or reduce brushmarks. For broad areas, lay off in a criss-cross fashion.

APPLYING PAINT WITH A ROLLER

Applying paint by roller can be the fastest and easiest way of painting, even though any task will still require some cutting in with a brush.

Make sure you cover or mask surfaces and areas not to be painted. Rollers have a tendency to splatter paint over a wide area if they are not used correctly. Also be aware that a roller sleeve will leave the surface with a slight texture which is different from that left by a brush. The texture may be noticeable if the wrong sleeve is used (see page 11).

1 Cut in around the edges of the area as necessary. To do this, use a brush to paint out about 75 mm from the edge so that you don't have to worry about the roller hitting surfaces that aren't being painted. Later, when you are applying paint with the roller, you should roll over

the cut-in area as close as you can to the edge without hitting it.

2 Place the roller tray in a convenient place so you do not have to reach too far.

3 Fill the roller tray but do not overfill it. The tray is designed to hold paint and still have a flat surface free of paint on which to remove excess paint from the roller.

4 Place the roller sleeve in the paint and then roll it firmly back and forth along the tray. This will evenly coat the sleeve with paint. If the coating is even, paint will not drip when the roller is lifted from the tray to the surface. Uneven loading, or using too little paint, will result in patchy application, while loading too much paint on the roller will make it skid over the surface.

5 Start about one roller width from the cut-in section and work towards the edge, going as close as possible to eliminate join marks.

6 Spread the paint evenly on the surface. Refill the roller and continue to spread paint evenly. Start each loaded roller one width away from the last and work back towards the already painted area. This avoids overloading the surface with paint, which can lead to a poor finish.

7 After applying two or three roller loads, run a relatively dry roller

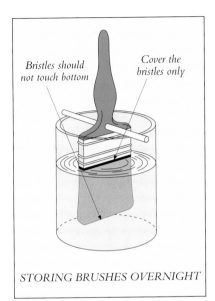

Bristles should not touch bottom

Cover the bristles only

STORING BRUSHES OVERNIGHT

lightly back over the just-painted area. This will remove any heavy texture or thick edges. Continue the above sequence until all the surface area is coated.

CLEANING BRUSHES
BRUSHES USED WITH EMULSION PAINTS

Brushes that have been used in water-based, or emulsion, paint should be cleaned thoroughly in water. Make sure all the paint is removed from up under the metal band, as any paint left will work its way out during future use. Rinse the brush in warm, soapy water, and then in clean water. Finally, spin the brush by holding the handle between the open palms of your hands and moving your hands back and forth quickly. The handle will turn in your hands, flicking out the excess material. Allow the brush to dry.

For environmental reasons, do not clean brushes in the sink. Use old pots or buckets when cleaning brushes in water and empty the waste water onto the garden.

BRUSHES USED WITH OIL-BASED PAINTS

If you have been using oil-based paint, your brush can be stored overnight or for short periods in water. Take care when doing this, however, as leaving a brush in water for too long will deform the bristles. It is best to suspend the brushes in the water by inserting a stick through a hole in the stock (see the diagram on page 15). Be sure to keep the depth of water equal to the length of the bristles, as any paint exposed to the air will harden.

When you have finished using the brush, clean it thoroughly before putting it away.

Brushes that have been used with oil-based paints are cleaned with white spirit, brush cleaner or turpentine. Use two containers with a small quantity of solvent in each.

1 Rinse the brush in the first pot to remove most of the paint, then spin out the solvent from the bristles by holding the handle between your hands and moving your hands back and forth quickly.

2 Place the brush in the second pot to rinse out the remaining paint. Remove and spin out the residue.

3 Rinse the brush in warm, soapy water to remove the solvent, and then rinse it in clean water and spin out the water from the bristles.

4 Dry the brush on a flat surface or hang it up to dry.

5 When you have cleaned the brushes, pour the dirty solvent into a container and store it. The residue paint will gradually settle to the bottom, leaving reusable solvent for the future. Even dirty solvent can be used for that first rinse. Old solvent should be disposed of at a suitable waste disposal depot.

CLEANING PAINT ROLLERS

Cleaning paint rollers can be one of the worst jobs, especially if the roller has been in oil-based paints. The most effective and efficient way is with a wire loop.

1 Place the wire loop over the sleeve and slide the loop slowly down the length of the sleeve, squeezing the excess paint back into the paint can or tray.

2 Pour a small amount of solvent or water, depending on the paint used, into the tray. Use the cutting-in brush to loosen and dissolve paint on the surface of the tray.

3 Place the roller in the tray and move it back and forth to clean it. Remove the roller from the tray, drain the solvent from the sleeve and pour excess solvent into a container.

4 Repeat the process with clean solvent. Depending on the colour of paint used, you may need to repeat the process another time for thorough cleaning.

5 Wash the sleeve in warm, soapy water, rinse it and spin it dry. Store the roller upright to avoid creating a flat spot on the sleeve.

1 To clean a roller, place a wire loop over the sleeve and slide it slowly down, squeezing out excess paint.

ALTERNATIVE METHODS FOR CLEANING ROLLERS

There are also several mechanical devices for cleaning rollers.
- Roller spinners are probably the easiest way to clean a roller. Place the end of the spinner in the hollow end of the roller's sleeve and hold both inside a large container such as an old drum or 20 litre paint can. Don't use a small container or paint will fly everywhere. Lift the handle of the spinner and plunge it down so that the roller spins and flicks the residue paint onto the inside walls of the container.
- Mechanical roller cleaning machines are also available for cleaning rollers used with water-based paint. The roller sleeve is placed in a plastic tube which is connected to a water hose. The force of the water entering the tube forces the roller to spin, and the constant flow of water thoroughly washes the paint from the sleeve.

Lift the roller spinner's handle and press down so that the sleeve spins and flicks off paint.

COMMON PAINT DEFECTS

BITTINESS (pieces of grit, dirt or dust on or in the painted surface)
- *Cause 1:* Dirty equipment. *Prevention:* Clean brushes or rollers.
- *Cause 2:* Painting in a dirty or dusty area or room. *Prevention:* Vacuum the area.
- *Cause 3:* Using old, unstrained paint. *Prevention:* Strain the paint through muslin or an old pair of stockings or tights.

BLEEDING (paint discoloured by some underlying substance)
- *Cause 1:* Surface coated with bitumen. *Prevention:* Use aluminium paint as a sealer.
- *Cause 2:* Surface contains dyestuffs. *Prevention:* Use shellac as a sealant before painting.

BLOOMING (a whitish look on the surface of varnish or enamel paint)
- *Cause 1:* Painting in cold or damp conditions. *Prevention:* Avoid application during this time.
- *Cause 2:* Painting in steamy or humid conditions. *Prevention:* Apply paint in dry conditions.

CISSING (paint rolls back in globules, leaving small bare patches)
- *Cause 1:* Painting over greasy surfaces. *Prevention:* Clean the surface thoroughly.
- *Cause 2:* Painting very shiny surfaces. *Prevention:* Abrade the surface to remove shine.

LIFTING (paint softens previous coating)
- *Cause 1:* Previous coating has not dried. *Prevention:* Allow adequate drying time.
- *Cause 2:* Previous coating is not resistant. *Prevention:* Ensure the new paint is compatible with the solvent in the old paint.

MISSES (patches where paint has not been applied)
- *Cause 1:* Careless application of paint. *Prevention:* Apply paint more carefully.
- *Cause 2:* Inadequate lighting. *Prevention:* Provide better lighting.
- *Cause 3:* Top coat colour too close to undercoat. *Prevention:* Use lighter undercoat.

ORANGE PEEL (textured finish that resembles the skin of an orange)
- *Cause:* Not laying off after using a roller (mainly occurs with gloss enamel). *Prevention:* Lay off with a paintbrush after rolling.

PEELING/FLAKING PAINT (paint does not adhere to the surface or coat of paint)
- *Cause 1:* Painting damp surfaces. *Prevention:* Ensure surface is dry and free of moisture.
- *Cause 2:* Painting powdery surfaces. *Prevention:* Prepare and seal surface correctly.

PEELING/FLAKING PAINT (*cont.*)
- *Cause 3:* Lack of adhesion on shiny surfaces. *Prevention:* Abrade the surface to remove shine.

BRUSHMARKS (marks in the surface of the paint coating; this defect reduces gloss level and will retain dirt)
- *Cause 1:* Poor application. *Prevention:* Apply paint correctly and lay off carefully.
- *Cause 2:* The finishing paint was applied over poorly applied undercoats. *Prevention:* Abrade the surface to remove brushmarks.

UNEVEN SHEEN (patches on flat or low-sheen finishes)
- *Cause 1:* Edge sets before the join is painted over. *Prevention:* Use appropriate equipment.
- *Cause 2:* Surface too porous, causing uneven drying. *Prevention:* Apply paint over a well-sealed or undercoated surface.

SLOW DRYING (paint is tacky after a long drying period)
- *Cause 1:* Grease or polish was not removed before painting. *Prevention:* Remove all the grease or polish.
- *Cause 2:* Not enough ventilation in the room. *Prevention:* Provide adequate ventilation.
- *Cause 3:* Too much tint in the paint. *Prevention:* Use an appropriate base colour and less tint.

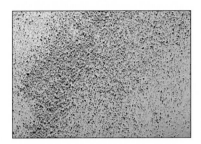

Bittiness (dirt in painted surface)

Cissing (paint rolls back)

Orange peel (textured finish)

Brushmarks (marks visible)

Clear coatings for floors

Clear finishes are ideal for highlighting the natural beauty of timber floors. They come in matt, satin or gloss finishes and can be water-based or solvent-based.

CLEAR COATINGS

Clear coatings are used for a number of reasons. They make the surface easy to clean, seal the timber from dirt and grime and make the surface more durable. They also reduce moisture penetration and protect the surface against scratches.

In order to choose the correct finishing system you must decide first if your floor will be stained or just clear-coated. Also consider how much wear and tear or foot traffic the floor will receive.

When selecting a finish, remember that a clear finish will darken the natural colour because it penetrates the timber to some degree. For example, when natural pine is coated with an oil-based clear finish, it deepens over time from a soft cream to a deep honey colour.

CLEAR FINISHES FOR INTERIOR FLOORS

• Polyurethanes are hard-wearing and suitable for all interior timbers, including floors. These coatings are

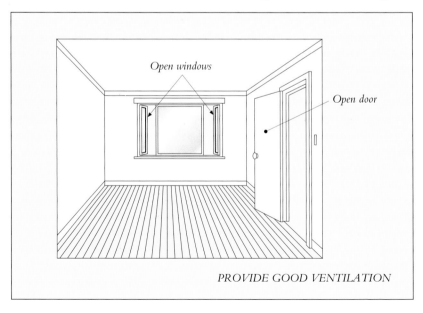

Open windows

Open door

PROVIDE GOOD VENTILATION

These four finishes were all applied to the same timber floor. Clockwise from top left: Danish oil finish, polyurethane satin clear coat, wax finish, and stained timber with clear coat.

resistant to heat and harsh chemicals. Polyurethanes are available in matt, satin and gloss finishes.

• Two-pack polyurethanes are extra-hard-wearing. They should not, however, be used over a coating of single-pack polyurethane as they will soften the first coating and lift it.

• Water-based clear coatings are available in a range of finishes. Some are specifically designed for floors and are as durable as their oil-based counterparts, if not more so. They provide a tough, non-yellowing coating which dries clear and so is perfect for light or blond timbers. These coatings are water-soluble, dry fast, and have less odour than oil-based finishes.

• Varnishes are oil-modified natural or synthetic resin-based finishes, which dry to a hard protective coating. Interior varnishes generally have a low oil content, and they come in matt, satin or gloss finishes. However, varnishes have, to a large part, been replaced by more modern water-based coatings and by polyurethane finishes.

• Sanding sealer is not designed as a finishing coat. Its purpose is to seal open-grained timber. It is fast-drying and can be applied to either bare or previously stained timber.

• Shellac is a natural, orange-coloured resin. Methylated spirit is its solvent. It is not suitable for light timbers if you want to retain the timber colour, because it will darken the timber. Shellac is a relatively soft finish that is not very durable.

TOOLS AND MATERIALS

• Preparation equipment (see page 6)
• Sanding sealer (optional)
• Clear finish of choice
• 50 mm flat brushes

APPLYING A CLEAR FINISH

1 Clean the surface to ensure it is free of dirt and grease. Allow it to dry completely.

2 Repair any surface faults or defects in the timber (see pages 6–9). Bleach out any stains or dark patches visible in the floorboards.

3 Smooth the surface, sanding with the grain. Vacuum the timber to remove all the dust.

4 Open all doors and windows to ensure there is adequate ventilation in the room while you are working.

5 Apply the appropriate clear finish (see the box opposite), following the manufacturer's recommendations on the container.

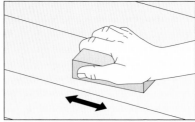

3 Sand the surface smooth, working in the direction of the grain, and then vacuum up all the dust.

SPECIFICATIONS FOR CLEAR COATINGS

Once you have decided which clear finish you want to use on your floor, read the manufacturer's instructions on the container carefully. The number of coats necessary and the order of application will vary according to the type of clear finish chosen.

CLEAR GLOSS (1)
Surface preparation: Repair faults, sand floor and dust down
First coat: Sanding sealer or polyurethane gloss
Second coat: Polyurethane gloss
Third coat: Polyurethane gloss

CLEAR GLOSS (2)
Surface preparation: Repair faults, sand floor and dust down
First coat: Two-pack polyurethane or water-based floor gloss
Second coat: Two-pack polyurethane or water-based floor gloss
Third coat: Optional third coat of the two-pack polyurethane or water-based gloss

CLEAR SATIN
Surface preparation: Repair faults, sand floor and dust down
First coat: Sanding sealer, satin polyurethane or water-based floor clear
Second coat: Satin polyurethane or water-based floor clear
Third coat: Optional third coat

CLEAR MATT
Surface preparation: Repair faults, sand floor and dust down
First coat: Polyurethane matt or water-based matt floor clear
Second coat: Polyurethane matt or water-based matt floor clear
Third coat: Optional third coat

STAIN AND CLEAR
Surface preparation: Repair faults, sand floor and dust down
First coat: Wood stain
Second coat: Clear polyurethane gloss, satin or matt
Third coat: Clear polyurethane gloss, satin or matt
Fourth coat: Optional fourth coat

ONE-STEP STAIN
Surface preparation: Repair faults, sand floor and dust down
First coat: Stain varnish
Second coat: Stain varnish
Third coat: Polyurethane or water-based clear coat

WATER-BASED STAIN AND CLEAR
Surface preparation: Repair faults, sand floor and dust down
First coat: Water-based stain
Second coat: Clear polyurethane or water-based clear
Third coat: Clear polyurethane or water-based clear
Fourth coat: Optional fourth coat

Applying a wax finish

Waxes are valued for the soft lustre they give to quality timber (see page 21) and the hard-wearing coating they provide for floors. Wax finishes come in both liquid and paste forms.

TOOLS AND MATERIALS

- Preparation equipment (see page 6)
- Wax finish
- Soft cloths
- 50 mm brush (if using liquid wax)

WAX FINISHES

Natural wax finishes can be applied either to bare timber or over timber that has already been coated with a sanding sealer, a polyurethane clear finish or a shellac.

Most wax finishes are a combination of carnauba wax (from the Brazilian wax palm) and beeswax. They are available as a clear polish or in a variety of timber colours. Some are perfumed with oils, such as eucalyptus, to give a pleasant scent.

Wax finishes are applied with a brush, if they are in liquid form, or a cloth pad. The wax is then buffed to give a subtle shine. This is hard work, and wax finishes have been largely replaced by more modern coatings that are quicker to apply.

METHOD

1 Prepare the timber floor (see pages 6–9), repairing any damage and bleaching out any stains. All defects will be visible through the wax finish, so work carefully and thoroughly at this stage. Sand and seal the floor as required. Allow it to dry thoroughly.

2 Apply the wax, if in paste form, with a soft cloth, using a circular movement. Use only a small amount at a time or circular marks will be visible when the wax hardens. If the wax is in liquid form, use a brush, working in the direction of the grain.

3 Wait 5 to 10 minutes for the wax to begin to harden. Repeat the process to build up the thickness of the wax coating.

4 Wipe off any excess wax and lightly rub over the floor with a soft cloth to give a sheen.

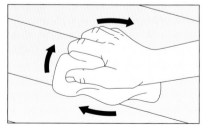

2 Apply a little of the wax at a time, using a soft cloth and working with a circular movement.

Applying an oil finish

Oil finishes are water-resistant, easy to apply and give a soft, smooth, usually hard-wearing finish to a timber floor. They are applied to bare timber.

OIL FINISHES

Tung oil is the most suitable oil finish for floors. Applying several coats – with a sanding between each – will give a hard-wearing surface.

Danish oil (also known as teak oil) is a polyurethane oil-based product used on bare timber. Polyurethane means that the drying time is much quicker than tung oil. It penetrates and seals timber, but is best suited to surfaces not subject to abrasion.

APPLYING TUNG OIL FINISH

1 Prepare the timber floor (see pages 6–9). Make sure that all traces of previous finishes and stains are removed, so that the oil can penetrate the grain effectively.

2 Apply the first coat of oil with the brush, working the oil into the timber and brushing with the grain.

HINT

The cloths used for oil rubbing must be disposed of in a container of water or laid out to dry before being stored. Otherwise it is possible they will catch fire through spontaneous combustion.

Use a clean, soft cloth to wipe away the excess oil (excess oil will dry slowly and cause a patchy, uneven sheen). Leave to dry for 24 hours.

3 Lightly sand the entire floor surface with fine silicon-carbide abrasive paper. Use a clean, soft cloth to apply the second coat of oil, rubbing with the timber grain. Wipe away excess oil and leave to dry for 24 hours.

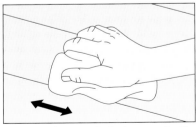

3 Use a clean, soft cloth to apply the second coat of oil, rubbing in the direction of the timber grain.

Staining a floor

A stain colours timber but does not offer protection. It will bring out the characteristics of the wood and can make a cheap timber look like something much more expensive (see page 21).

TOOLS AND MATERIALS

- Preparation equipment (see page 6)
- Turpentine
- Stain
- 50 mm flat brush
- Sanding sealer (optional)
- Clear finish

METHOD

1 Prepare the floor (see pages 6–9). If you need to use wood filler, read the instructions carefully as you may need to apply it before or after the first application of stain. This will depend on the filler type.

2 Clean the timber thoroughly with turpentine. Make sure all grease, dirt and dust have been removed. Allow the floor to dry.

3 Find a scrap piece of floorboard that matches the boards you will be staining, and test the stain colour on it to judge the final appearance.

4 Apply the stain, painting with the grain. Work along a few boards at a time, being careful not to go onto adjoining boards so that joins in the work will not be visible. Allow the stain to dry.

5 If you like, you can now apply sanding sealer over the stain. Allow it to dry. Sand again.

6 Apply a coat of clear finish (see pages 20–3). Allow it to dry and then lightly sand the floorboards.

7 Apply a second and further coats of clear finish as desired.

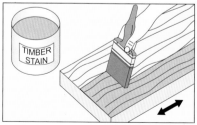

3 Find a scrap of timber that matches your floorboards and test the stain colour on it.

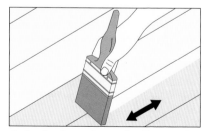

4 Apply the stain to the floor, using a brush and painting in the direction of the grain.

TYPES OF STAINS

There are a number of different types of stain to use, depending on your particular requirements. Each is based on a different medium to enable the pigment to penetrate the wood. This medium can be water, spirit, oil or varnish.

Stains can be almost transparent, changing the colour of the timber only slightly, or they can alter the colour of the timber while still allowing the grain to show through. Stains can also be so dark that the grain in the timber is almost hidden. The depth of colour you choose will depend partly on the condition of your floorboards (if they are in poor condition you may want to use a really dark stain) and partly on the effect you want to achieve.

All stains must be applied to clean, bare wood that has been wiped down beforehand with turpentine. Always follow the manufacturer's instructions.

OIL STAIN
Composition: Pigments in oil or synthetic resin
Solvent: Turpentine
Advantages: Ideal for applying to softwoods; easy to apply; gives an even finish
Disadvantages: Slow-drying

SPIRIT STAIN
Composition: Dyes in shellac thinned with methylated spirits
Solvent: Methylated spirits
Advantages: Best on oily or hard, fine-grained timber; gives a good base for French polishing
Disadvantages: Fast-drying

VARNISH STAIN
Composition: Oil stain and hard-drying oil varnish
Solvent: Turpentine
Advantages: Suitable for most timbers; allows easy two-coat application
Disadvantages: A smooth finish is difficult to achieve

WATER STAIN
Composition: Pigments dissolved in boiling water
Solvent: Water
Advantages: Easy to apply; large colour range; looks best on close-grained timbers
Disadvantages: May give uneven finish on softwoods; as it is a water-based coating, it will lift the timber grain

WAX STAIN
Composition: Pigments in beeswax or paraffin wax
Solvent: Turpentine
Advantages: Not difficult to apply; gives a soft, antique look
Disadvantages: Very hard work to apply; cannot have a clear coat added to give extra protection to the floor

This simple stained pattern will add interest to a floor while retaining the formal appearance of the room. Only three coloured stains were used, with the centre circle left unstained.

Imitation parquet floor

A light timber floor with a clear coating can be decorated with a number of darker timber stains to produce an effect that resembles inlay work. The number of stains used and the intricacy of the design are up to you.

TOOLS AND MATERIALS

- Preparation equipment (see page 6)
- Clear polyurethane satin finish
- Chalk line and large set square
- Low-tack masking tape
- Stains: walnut, maple and oak
- Lint-free cloths

METHOD

1 Prepare the floor (see pages 6–9), and then apply one coat of clear finish. Allow it to dry thoroughly.

2 Find the centre of the floor and use a chalk line to mark diagonals to each corner of the room. Measure 300 mm from the centre along each diagonal; join the points to form the square. Make a cardboard template of the square and turn it to form the underlying diamond shape. From the centre draw a circle 1 m in diameter. Decide on the position of the corner squares; measure out the distance along the diagonals. Measure another 220 mm and use a set square to draw a perpendicular line across the diagonal. Measure a further 220 mm on the diagonal and on each arm, and connect the points to form a square.

3 Tape around all the areas marked '1' in the photograph below and, using lint-free cloths, apply walnut stain. Don't use a brush as it may overload the area, and the stain may creep under the masking tape. Remove the tape and allow the stain to dry. Repeat using the maple stain for areas marked '2'.

4 Apply a thin coat of clear finish over the centre circle and the newly stained sections. Allow it to dry.

5 Mask the coated areas, and apply oak stain to the rest of the floor. Allow it to dry. Apply a coat of clear finish over the entire floor.

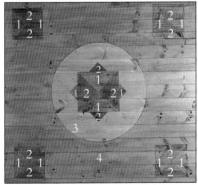

Key: 1 = walnut stain, 2 = maple stain, 3 = unstained, 4 = oak stain

Painted floor rug

Painting a floor to look like a rug will add character to your home. Make sure the design suits the location and condition of your floorboards, and choose colours that are in harmony with the existing decor.

PLANNING

This rug has stencilled designs on a sponged ground. You can use water- or oil-based paints, but water-based ones are easier to apply and are quick-drying. A final clear coat is given to protect the paint and enhance the colours. The finish is opaque, and so no wood grain shows through.

You can adapt the colours and size of the pattern to suit your room, or you can use the same techniques to create a completely different design. There is plenty of scope for imagination. Books or brochures on designer and antique rugs will provide inspiration. Use colours that blend with your furnishings for a custom-made look.

PREPARATION

1 Mark out the area of the rug (1500 x 1060 mm), using a tape measure and chalk line.

2 Lightly sand inside the marked lines using abrasive paper wrapped around a sanding block. Clean away the dust. If the floorboards have a wax coating, remove it using a wax stripping product; follow the manufacturer's instructions.

3 Apply the undercoat. If you are painting over unpainted or new

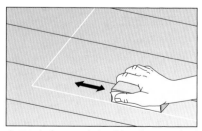

2 Lightly sand inside the marked lines, using abrasive paper and a cork sanding block.

The light background colour of this cheery painted rug shows up well against the dark floorboards. A darker background would have been necessary if the boards were light–coloured.

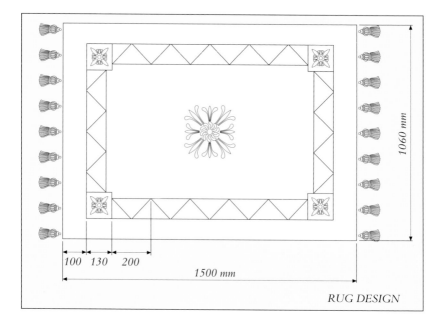

1060 mm

100 130   200

1500 mm

RUG DESIGN

boards, use a water-based primer undercoat. If the floor has been clear-coated with an oil-based finish, you will need to lightly sand and apply an oil-based undercoat. Allow to dry.

4 Lightly sand and apply the base colour (cream). Allow 4 hours for it to dry.

5 Create a darker tone and a lighter tint of the base colour by mixing in a little black (or grey) and white respectively. Apply the darker colour using a damp natural sea sponge, working evenly over the surface in a random fashion. Allow it to dry. Apply the lighter colour using the same technique, making sure the base colour and the darker tone show through. Allow to dry.

6 Measure 100 mm in from the edge of the rug and mark a line. This is the guideline for the triangular border pattern. Mark out the corner squares and paint the outline.

STENCILLING

7 Enlarge the triangular pattern opposite onto medium-weight card. Cut out the shaded section and coat

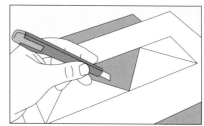

7 Enlarge the triangular pattern onto medium-weight card and cut out the shaded section.

32

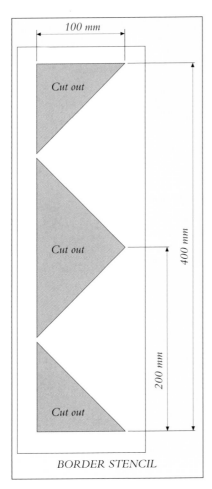

100 mm

Cut out

400 mm

Cut out

200 mm

Cut out

BORDER STENCIL

9 Reverse the stencil and fill in the other triangular areas with red paint. Allow to dry.

10 Mark off the positions for the tassels, making sure you space them evenly. Stencil them using a roller and the base colour paint (cream).

11 Centre the flower template on the corner squares and apply red paint using a roller. Allow to dry.

12 Place the sunburst stencil in the centre of the rug and use the roller to apply red paint. Allow to dry and then apply the blue. Sponge over the centre parts to give a mottled effect.

13 To protect the painting apply one or two coats of clear finish (to match the surrounding floor).

This effect was created using only three colours: cream, red and blue.

the stencil with shellac. Enlarge the designs for the sunburst, the flower and the tassel (all on page 60) on a photocopier. Transfer them to card, cut out the designs and seal the stencils with shellac (see page 43).

8 Align the triangle stencil against the inside of the marked line and fill in the colour, using a small foam roller and blue paint. Allow to dry.

An open pattern of coloured squares was used on this limewashed floor, but a more regular checkerboard pattern would be equally effective. The colour chosen could pick up a tone from the walls or soft furnishings.

Limewashed floor

The limewashed finish on this timber floor has been enhanced by a pattern of green squares arranged diagonally across the room. For a more formal look, the squares could have been aligned parallel to the walls.

TOOLS AND MATERIALS

- Preparation equipment (see page 6)
- Satin clear finish
- 100 mm and 50 mm flat brushes
- Tape measure and pencil
- Chalk line
- Low-tack masking tape
- Water-based liming finish in white
- Green liming finish or paint (or desired colour)

LIME FINISHES

Traditionally, liming involved brushing a coat of lime over a timber surface and then wiping it off so that some lime remained in the timber grain. This process was used in the sixteenth century to clean and protect timber against woodworm, but the ingrained lime produced a decorative finish that became popular for its own sake.

The process has changed over the years, which is just as well – the use of lime can damage skin and the respiratory system.

Modern liming mixtures consist of a translucent glaze or an opaque grain-filling pigment. They can be white or coloured.

Lime finishes are pre-mixed by various paint manufacturers and are ready for use over bare or stained timbers. Alternatively, you can prepare your own, using either oil-based or water-based paints. The materials and process you use will be determined by the type of timber in your floor – hardwood or softwood – and its condition.

PREPARATION

1 Establish whether your floor is made from hardwood or softwood. Hardwood is generally open-grained, while softwoods have a closed grain. If you have hardwood floors, ensure the open grain is clear of all previous coatings. Stubborn paint should be removed with a liquid paint remover and a wire brush.

2 Repair the floor (see pages 6–9) and then sweep and vacuum the area to remove all the dust and debris.

HINT

Before applying any liming finish, use a sample piece of floor timber to test your technique, the colour and the setting time.

MIXING YOUR OWN LIMING MEDIUMS

The mixtures suggested below are a guide only. Test them on a scrap piece of timber and adjust them to suit your timber before beginning work on the floor.

OIL-BASED MIX
This is suitable for use on hardwoods (open-grain timbers). It consists of:
5 parts white oil-based undercoat
1 part linseed oil
2 parts turpentine

WATER-BASED MIX
This is suitable for both open- and closed-grain timbers.
3 parts white flat emulsion paint
1 part water-based glaze medium
1 part water

Sand the area, working with the grain. Remove the dust.

3 Apply a thin coat of clear finish over the timber, taking care not to fill the open grain or you will later lose the effect of the limewash.

APPLYING THE PATTERN
4 Find the centre of the room and use a chalk line to mark two intersecting lines parallel to the walls. Measure 170 mm along each and connect the points to form a square 240 mm on each side.

5 Continue the lines formed by each side of the square to the edge of the room. Measure 400 mm (or an appropriate distance) along each line and then mark in three 240 mm squares as shown in the diagram opposite. Add a square on either side of the middle of the three squares. Repeat this step until you are close to the corners of the room.

6 If your room is large enough, add in further squares by extending the lines as required. Place a square in each corner of the room.

7 Mask around the inside edge of the coloured squares using low-tack masking tape.

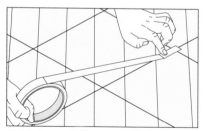

7 *Mask carefully around the inside of the coloured squares using low-tack masking tape.*

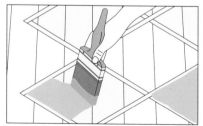

10 *Mask around the remaining squares and repeat the liming with the coloured mixture.*

8 Using a brush, apply the white limewash to the floor except for the masked-off squares. If you are using a pre-mixed finish, work according to the manufacturer's instructions. Allow the limewash to dry. If the colour is not deep enough, add another coat.

9 Apply a thin coat of clear finish over the paint, remove the masking tape and allow the floor to dry.

10 Mask around the remaining squares using low-tack masking tape. Repeat the liming with the coloured

HINT

Liming on commercial furniture is generally applied by spray. It is very difficult to match this finish at home when using conventional liming methods.

mixture. Remove the tape. If any of the mixture has crept under the tape, wipe it off before it dries. Allow the floor to dry.

11 When the floor is completely dry, apply two coats of satin clear floor finish.

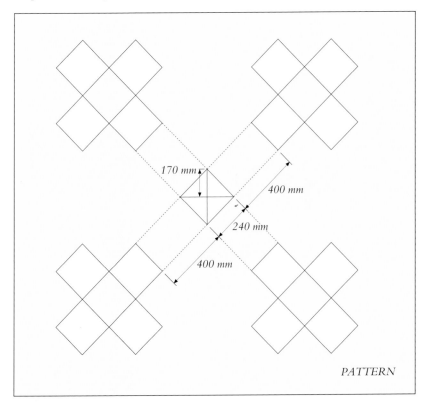

170 mm

400 mm

240 mm

400 mm

PATTERN

37

Crackle-effect floor

Crackling occurs naturally in a painted surface when the paint is stressed as a result of structural movement, humidity or the use of incompatible paint mediums. The effect is, however, attractive and can be created artificially.

TOOLS AND MATERIALS

- Preparation equipment (see page 6)
- Clear finish
- Paint: medium blue and pale lavender (or colours of choice)
- Crackle medium
- 100 mm flat brushes

CRACKLE FINISHES

There are various ways of obtaining a crackle effect. The principle is that you apply a fast-drying paint over a still damp, slow-drying paint.

Today there are crackle mediums to help achieve the look. Different products produce different degrees of crackling, as does the thickness of the application. A thin coat of paint over a thick coat of crackle medium will result in large cracks, whereas a thick coat of paint over a thin coat of crackle medium will produce small cracks. Experiment a little first to get the result you want.

This is an opaque finish, so little or no timber colour will be evident.

METHOD

1 Sand new floorboards, remove the dust and apply a clear coat to seal the surface (see pages 6–9). Clean old clear-coated boards, lightly sand them and then dust.

2 Apply the base coat (medium blue) evenly over the floor. Allow to dry.

3 Brush on an even coat of crackle medium and allow it to dry. Drying time will vary depending on the

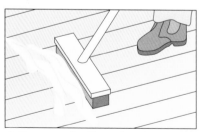

1 Prepare the floor by cleaning it thoroughly and then adding a coat of sealer if the boards are new.

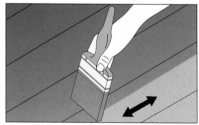

3 Brush an even coat of crackle medium over the base coat and allow it to dry.

A dark base colour and lighter top colour give the most effective aged look. Here a pale lavender was used over a medium blue base.

thickness of application and air circulation in the room. The manufacturer's instructions on the product should give you an idea.

4 Gently paint on the contrasting top coat, disturbing the crackle layer as little as possible. The crackle process will begin almost immediately as the top coat contracts and the base coat begins to show through.

5 Apply one or two coats of clear finish. Use matt, satin or gloss to match the surrounding paint finishes and traffic conditions.

A simple foliage pattern was used over a limewashed base to create this elegant floor. The stencil was reversed for each alternate use to vary the design, and three shades of green were used to give a lifelike result.

Stencilled floor

Stencilling is one of the easiest ways to decorate a floor, and the technique is the same whatever design you choose and whether you are stencilling over a painted or clear finish. Sponge applicators were used to create subtle colour effects on this floor.

TOOLS AND MATERIALS

- Preparation equipment (see page 6)
- White paint or limewash
- Clear finish
- 100 mm flat brush or paint roller
- Graph paper
- Chalk line or timber straight edge
- Medium-weight card and craft knife
- Shellac
- Green paint in three shades
- Sponge applicators (see page 43)
- Low-tack masking tape

PREPARATION

1 Ensure the floor is clean and in good repair, and then lightly sand and dust it down (see pages 6–9). Apply a base coat of white paint or limewash or, if you prefer, a coat of clear finish. Allow it to dry.

2 Set out the floor plan of the room on graph paper. This will allow you to work out the design and adjust it until you are happy with it. The floor in the photograph was based on a 400 mm grid, but you can adjust it to suit your room. Start from the centre of the room so that the design in the centre is appropriately placed.

3 Mark out the grid on the floor, using a chalk line or a straight length of timber. These lines will guide you when placing the stencil.

4 Enlarge and prepare the foliage stencil (see pages 61 and 43).

STENCILLING

5 Centre the stencil over the guide line. For each side of a square, use the stencil once and then reverse it and stencil again. Work from the centre of the line to the corner of the square. In order to achieve a subtle, flowing result, work with three shades of green, using the darkest shade for the stems and largest leaves, and the lightest for the new growth on the ends. Apply the paint with sponge applicators, which will enable

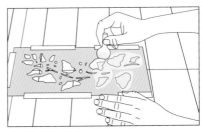

5 Use homemade sponge applicators to apply the paint and slowly build up the opacity you require.

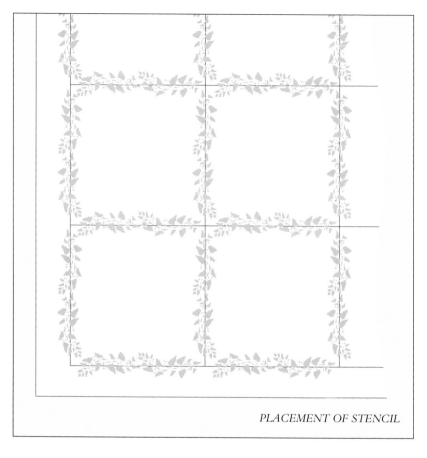

PLACEMENT OF STENCIL

you to apply all three shades using the same stencil.

6 Keep a supply of rags handy and use them to clean up the edges where necessary. Carefully wipe under the stencil each time before you reverse it. This will reduce the risk of smudging.

7 Allow the design to dry for 12 hours before applying at least two coats of a matt, satin or gloss water-based or oil-based clear finish to protect the painting.

6 Use a rag to clean up the edges regularly and to wipe under the stencil to reduce the risk of smudging.

STENCILLING

MAKING A STENCIL
A serviceable stencil can be made from medium-weight cardboard.

1 Enlarge the design to its full size, either on a photocopier or by the grid method. For example, draw a 1 cm grid over the design and then draw a 2 cm grid on a clean sheet of paper. Draw the lines within each square of the original into the larger squares.

2 Copy the design onto the cardboard, either by rubbing pencil on the back of the design and tracing over the lines or using carbon paper. Cut out the stencil using a craft or utility knife.

3 Coat the stencil with shellac to seal the card, keep the edges of the cut-out areas sharp and stop them fraying. This also makes cleaning easier.

USING A STENCIL
Position the stencil carefully and use low-tack masking tape to secure it. Apply the paint and then carefully lift off the stencil. Do not slide it over the paint or you will smudge the design.

USING A SMALL ROLLER
The quickest way to apply paint is to use a small foam roller (see the illustrations on pages 46 and 57).

This allows the paint to be spread evenly over the stencil.

Use an almost dry roller and slowly build up the paint until you get the coverage you want. If you use too much paint, it can seep under the stencil and smudge.

USING SPONGE APPLICATORS
A simple applicator can be made by cutting a strip from a bathroom sponge and folding it over. Use masking tape to tape around one end to form a handle. Applicators can be washed out or discarded once the job is complete.

Applicators allow you to apply several different colours of paint using the same stencil, and so are ideal for designs such as the foliage stencil on page 40. Do not apply too much paint at once, but slowly build up the colour you require.

STENCILLING FLOORS
Stencilling a floor requires the same process as any other stencilling, but you will find you have a tendency to apply heavier pressure (and, therefore, more paint) when you are bending over. This can cause the paint to creep under the stencil, resulting in smudges and ugly edges.

You will find that stencilling a floor is a strain on your back. Don't work over too large an area at once, and take regular breaks.

Mock terracotta tiles

Overlaying an existing floor with sheets of MDF is a simple way of covering rough floors and eliminating floorboard grooves and gaps. The smooth board is an ideal base for painted tiles.

PREPARATION

1 Measure and cut the MDF sheets to cover the floor. Seal the sheets. Use a liquid adhesive or equivalent to fix the MDF sheets to the floor, and then secure them with a few randomly spaced screws. Countersink the screws.

2 Give the floor a light sand. Fill the screw holes and the joints where the sheets join. Sand smooth when dry.

PAINTING THE FLOOR

3 Using a paint roller or 100 mm brush, apply an off-white base coat. This will also form the mortar joints.

4 Once the surface is dry, mark out the 300 mm square tiles, using a chalk line. To add the inlay tiles, measure out 75 mm along the grid lines and connect these points to make 100 mm squares. Use 8 mm

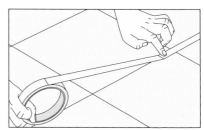

4 Mask along the chalk lines using 8 mm wide masking tape. This will create the mortar joints.

Painted terracotta tiles turn this MDF sheeting into an attractive floor, and the flower-patterned inlay tiles add extra interest. The colour and design of the inlay tiles can be varied to suit your decor.

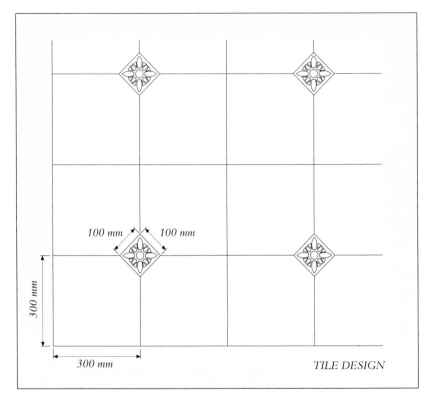

100 mm ⟋ ⟍ 100 mm

300 mm

300 mm

TILE DESIGN

wide masking tape to mask along the chalk lines. This will create the mortar joints between the tiles when the tape is removed. Mask around the inlay tiles.

5 Paint two coats of terracotta colour over the sheets. Then mix a lighter tint of terracotta colour by adding a little white to the paint. Use a damp sea sponge to dab some of the lighter

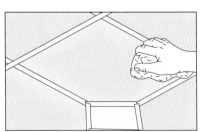

5 Mix a lighter tint of terracotta and use a damp sponge to dab around the inside edge of each tile.

6 When the blue paint is dry, add the flower, using the stencil, a small foam roller and white paint.

colour around the inside edge of each square to create contrast.

6 Paint the inlay tiles in blue. Before the paint is totally dry remove all the masking tape strips. After about 12 hours, stencil the centre of the inlay tiles, using the flower stencil on page 60, the small foam roller and white paint. See 'Stencilling' on page 43. Ensure the stencil is square and centred. Allow to dry.

7 Apply two coats of water-based clear finish. Satin will give the best finish, but choose a coating that is appropriate to your decor and the traffic conditions.

MEDIUM-DENSITY FIBREBOARD (MDF)

MDF is a resin-bonded wood fibre material with a smooth surface and an edge profile of uniform density. It is widely available and comes in a variety of ready-cut sheet sizes; a common size is 2400 x 1200 mm.

MDF FLOORS
MDF is used predominantly in the manufacturing of furniture, but can also be used as a flooring overlay. It can be painted, provided the surface is in good condition and the boards are not exposed to excessive moisture.

MDF is not waterproof and, therefore, must be completely sealed before it is laid. If it is not properly sealed the fibres will absorb moisture and swell. The durability of MDF in any area where moisture may be a problem is solely dependent on the quality of the sealing job. If the seal is broken – by a scratch or a chip that exposes the underlying fibres – an immediate repair must be made.

Fix MDF to existing timber floors with staples, nails or screws. MDF manufacturers recommend using parallel-threaded screws.

Most liquid adhesives are suitable for use on MDF. The choice of adhesive is determined by the surface characteristics and porosity of the other material being bonded, the application method and the bonding conditions. Always follow the manufacturer's recommendations in order to choose the right liquid adhesive for your job.

SEALING MDF
Seal all exposed surfaces and edges before laying the sheets; this undercoat is critical to a good finish. If smoothness is important, apply a solvent- or turpentine-based oil undercoat. Water-based sealer can be used, but it will cause some surface roughening and will have to be given additional sanding. Apply it according to the manufacturer's instructions.

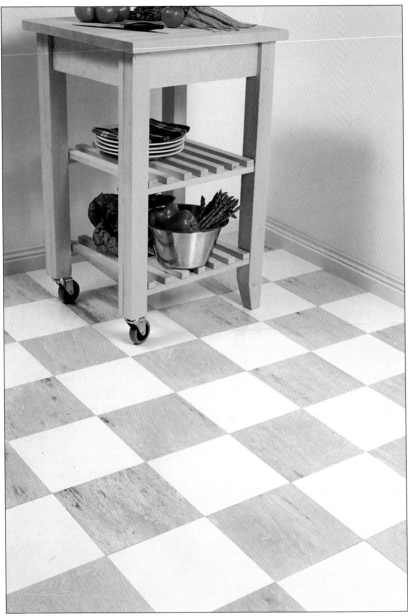

These MDF tiles were painted, half in plain white and half in granite finish, to create a very effective checkerboard floor. The tiles could, however, have been laid in any pattern desired.

Imitation granite tiles

For this floor MDF sheets were cut into tiles and painted plain white or given a granite finish. The technique used for the granite tiles is not difficult, and it can also be used with grey glaze to produce a marble effect.

THE GRANITE EFFECT

The technique used to create a granite-look finish is the same as that used to imitate marble or any similar stone. This effect is best suited to horizontal surfaces such as floors and table tops.

The effect is achieved using several glazes, dabbing and sponging them and then flicking turpentine or methylated spirits over the still-wet glaze. As simple as this sounds, the result is quite realistic.

As with any painted floor, the granite tiles will stand up to normal foot traffic as long as you give them two or three coats of clear finish.

PREPARATION

1 Measure the area precisely. On graph paper mark out your floor area and use this to work out which size of tiles will give you the look you want and best fit the room. Granite tiles usually measure 300 x 300 mm, but you may find that this is too large for your room. Scale them down if this is the case. Tiles that are 240 mm square may be most economical as you will then get 50 tiles from each 2400 x 1200 mm sheet of MDF. Calculate how many tiles you will need to cover your room and how many of each colour for your pattern.

2 Once the number of tiles and their size has been determined, you will

HINT

The glaze recipes given here are for horizontal surfaces such as floors. Don't use the same ratios for vertical surfaces, such as walls, as the paint will run.

need to cut them. If you feel uncomfortable cutting them yourself, ask your timber supplier to cut them. They may charge for this service.

3 Seal the MDF tiles (see the box on page 47). Lay the tiles out dry, butted against each other, and use a roller to paint on the base coat, using white low-sheen, water-based paint. Allow the paint to dry.

4 Paint the tiles that are to be white with two more coats of low-sheen white, and then finish them with at least two coats of water-based clear finish. (An oil-based finish will make the white look yellow.)

5 Collect the tiles that are to have the granite finish. You will need to

apply the paint to them quickly, so work on four tiles at a time and butt them up against one another to form a square. It's a good idea to practise on a spare tile first so that you achieve the look you want.

6 Mix the two glazes.
• Mid-grey. Mix 1 part white satin, oil-based paint to 2 parts turpentine and tint this with black to make a mid-grey.
• Grey/green. Mix 1 part white satin, oil-based paint to 2 parts turpentine and tint with green and a little black.

CREATING THE EFFECT
7 Brush a thin coat of clear glaze medium over the face of the tiles.

8 Dip a flat brush in the grey/green glaze. Gently tap the brush on the inside of the paint pot to remove excess paint. Dab and brush over 60 per cent of the surface of the tiles in an uneven chequered pattern.

9 Dip the flat brush into the grey glaze and remove excess paint. Dab

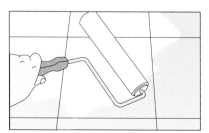

3 Lay the tiles out, butted against each other, and use a roller to paint on the base coat.

4 Paint the tiles that are to remain white with two coats of white low-sheen paint.

and brush into the remaining white spaces. Don't be concerned if you touch or mix colours, but work quickly. Throughout the process, work right to the edge of the tile or it will look as though it has a frame around it. Real granite tiles have been cut from large slabs, and the colour, texture and pattern travel well past the edges of the tile.

10 Soak the sea sponge in water, then squeeze out the excess. This will make the sponge soft and pliable so that it is easier to work with and to clean. Use the damp sponge to gently dab and disperse the colours. Try to eliminate any obvious pattern of colour. At this point you can lay the plastic bag onto the glaze and lift it off to vary the dappled look, but this is not essential.

11 Take the turpentine and dip the small brush into it. Tap the brush against the side of the container to remove the excess. Hold the brush over the tiles and rub a finger over the bristle. This will flick solvent onto the surface. The glazed surface will begin to ciss, creating various-sized holes and exposing the colour underneath. Repeat this process using methylated spirits.

12 Use the tissue paper and rag to gently dab the surface. This will mop up any large puddles of solvent. Set the tiles aside to dry overnight.

13 Repeat the process until all the tiles are painted.

TO FINISH
14 Protect the tiles with two or three coats of satin or gloss oil-based clear finish (whichever matches the finish on the white tiles), sanding lightly between coats.

15 Once the tiles have dried they can be fixed in place. Use a liquid adhesive and butt them tightly together. Begin laying them from one corner of the room.

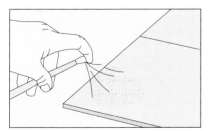

11 Hold the brush over the tiles and rub a finger over the bristle, flicking solvent onto the surface.

SPONGING TIPS

• Always use a natural sea sponge, as the holes have greater variation in shape and size.
• Wet the sponge thoroughly and then squeeze it out so it is soft and pliable.
• Before applying the sponge to the floor, always dab it a few times on a clean piece of paper to remove excess paint.
• When working, keep your hand moving and don't work over the same area twice.

Mock limestone blocks

Taking a bland concrete floor and transforming it to look like stone is not as big a challenge as you might think. The natural look and often uneven texture of a concrete floor enhances the painted stone effect.

TOOLS AND MATERIALS

- Stiff broom, vacuum cleaner and water blaster
- Tape measure and pencil
- Paving paints: cream, soft grey, soft lilac, beige, mid-grey
- 50 mm flat brush and small stiff brush
- Turpentine
- Natural sea sponge

METHOD

1 Clean the surface thoroughly (see page 9), first with a stiff broom, then a vacuum cleaner. If possible, use a high-pressure water blaster.

2 Mark out the blocks with a pencil, allowing a 10 mm gap between each of them for the joint.

3 Fill in the blocks using cream paving paint. Allow to dry according to the manufacturer's instructions.

4 Dilute the soft grey, beige and soft lilac paints with about 15 per cent turpentine.

5 Randomly brush on the various colours, leaving areas of cream showing through.

6 Use a damp sea sponge or lint-free cloth to dab and blend the colours together. When you are satisfied with the look, move on to the next block. Allow to dry.

7 Paint in the grout joints, using mid-grey paint and a small stiff brush. Try to be as accurate as possible.

3 Draw in the lines around each block and brush in the shapes using cream paving paint.

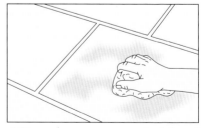

6 Use a damp sea sponge to dab and blend the colours together, working on one block at a time.

Blend two or three colours over a cream base to create the limestone blocks, varying the colours to suit your decor. If the 'grout' is a bit uneven it will add to the character of the work and make it look more natural.

Four colours are used in this tessellated design, with the lightest, cream, used as the base so that the pattern does not appear to be too heavy. Using the lightest colour as the base also reduces the amount of masking necessary.

Painted tessellated tiles

A smooth concrete surface is an ideal base for a painted tessellated tile design. Tessellated tile designs can be complicated, but the process described here can be easily reproduced.

CHOOSING PAINTS

Specifically manufactured paving or concrete paints are best for use on external surfaces such as verandahs, which may be subject to wet weather. These paints are now available in a wide range of colours so that you are able to re-create any number of interesting designs.

PREPARATION

1 Decide on the area you want to paint and whether to decorate all of it or only part. Tessellated tile floors consist of many small tiles, and so to reproduce the look you will need quite a long time and a lot of patience. The pattern used for this floor is relatively simple and uses four colours – cream, dark green, mid-green and dark red. The mid-green can be purchased or made by adding white to the dark green.

2 Prepare the concrete surface (see the box on page 9). If the surface is new, ensure it has a steel float finish. This provides a smooth surface for the paint. If the surface has been finished with a wooden float or broom, you will have to cover the textured finish before you begin painting. There are levelling products available that provide a perfect bond and a smooth surface on which to paint. Ask about them at your local hardware or DIY store. Allow at least 20 days for new concrete to dry thoroughly before you begin painting with oil-based paint.

3 Using a chalk line and tape measure, mark out the area to be painted (2500 x 1600 mm as here, or to suit your location).

4 Paint the marked area in the lightest colour, in this example cream. Apply two coats, allowing the

50 mm

40 mm

PATTERN

area to dry between coats. Be sure to follow the manufacturer's recommendations on the paint can.

CREATING THE DESIGN

5 Place 18 mm low-tack masking tape around the edge of the painted area, covering what will be the cream border. Measure in 140 mm and mark a line. Mask around on the line to form what will be the 140 mm wide dark green band. Paint in the band using dark green paint and the 75 mm brush, remove the tape and allow to dry.

6 From the green band, measure in 50 mm from the two short sides and 40 mm from the long sides, and draw guidelines.

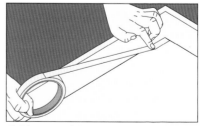

5 Place masking tape over the cream border, measure in 140 mm and mask to create the dark green border area.

7 Enlarge the designs and prepare the four stencils on page 62 and the flower stencil on page 60. Use medium-weight cardboard and coat the stencils with shellac (see the box Stencilling on page 43).

8 Place Tile stencil 1 in the corner of the cream area so that the points touch the guidelines. Using a foam roller, apply dark green paint. Move the stencil across (leaving 40 mm between the points) and repeat until the row is complete. Leaving 50 mm between the rows, repeat until the area is covered. Allow to dry.

9 Again starting in the top left-hand corner, position Tile stencil 2 and add the mid-green areas to each design. Allow to dry. Repeat with Tile stencil 3 and the dark red paint. Allow to dry.

10 Using Tile stencil 4, add the red diamonds to the dark green border. Work from either end of each side so that any uneven space occurs in the middle. If there is a small gap left, fill it with a small diamond (use Tile stencil 3 and mid-green paint), or for a larger gap place a red diamond in the centre and a small green one on either side of it.

11 Using the flower stencil and cream paint, add the flower design to the dark green diamond at the centre of each motif. Then add the flower to the red diamonds on the border at each corner and every fourth or fifth tile as appropriate (space them evenly). Again, start from the corners and work in.

TO FINISH
12 Using a grey pencil and ruler draw in simulated grout lines. This will help clean up the edges of each area of colour.

13 To seal the pencil you will have to give the surface two coats of oil-based clear coating in a satin finish. This will dull down over time to give a perfect finish, and it does protect the painting. However, applying a clear coating will take away the non-slip properties of the paving paint.

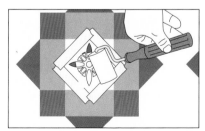

11 Stencil the flower design on the dark green diamond in the centre of each motif.

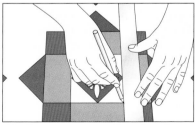

12 Use a grey pencil and ruler to draw in simulated grout lines around each area of colour.

Faux marble tiles

This simple faux marble effect will rejuvenate an old tiled floor, and if your tiles are on the larger side – 150 x 150 mm or more – they will appear more authentic.

TOOLS AND MATERIALS

- Tile primer (to etch surface)
- Satin enamel paints: white and black
- Turpentine
- 50 mm flat brushes
- Natural sea sponge or lint-free cloth
- Softener brush
- Satin clear finish and sanding equipment
- Grey grout

PLANNING
This project may take several days to complete, as many as five if you use oil-based paints.

METHOD
1 Ensure the tiles are free of any soap residue. Give the surface a thorough clean and rinse. Allow it to dry.

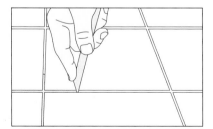

2 Using a large nail or scalpel, rake out most of the old grout from between the tiles.

Check the whole area for any loose tiles, and repair them.

2 Using any pointed tool, rake out most of the grout between the tiles.

3 Apply a coat of tile primer, which will allow the later coats of paint to bond with the surface. Follow the manufacturer's instructions.

4 Apply a base coat of white satin enamel and allow it to dry overnight.

5 Prepare the two glaze mixtures. If you use water-based paints, substitute water for the turpentine.
- White. Mix 4 parts white satin enamel and 1 part turpentine.
- Mid-grey. Mix 4 parts white satin enamel tinted with black and 1 part turpentine.

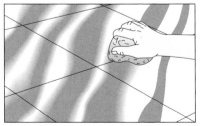

6 Use a damp sea sponge to blend the white and grey colours together, leaving some white base exposed.

The marble pattern painted on these tiles has turned a rather stark bathroom into something special. Plain white tiles formed an ideal base for the work.

6 Working on only one or two tiles at once, brush on the white glaze. While it is still wet, randomly brush on some mid-grey glaze. Use a damp sea sponge or lint-free cloth to blend the two colours together, leaving some areas of white exposed. Gently brush the surface with the bristle tips of a softener brush. This will blur the paint and give an illusion of depth to the finish. Repeat the process over all the tiles and allow to dry.

7 Paint on two or three coats of satin clear finish, lightly sanding between coats. Allow to dry thoroughly.

8 Following the manufacturer's instructions, re-grout the tiles with grey grout.

Stencils

*Sunburst stencil
(enlarge 225%)*

*Flower stencil
(enlarge 200%)*

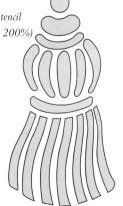

*Tassel stencil
(enlarge 200%)*

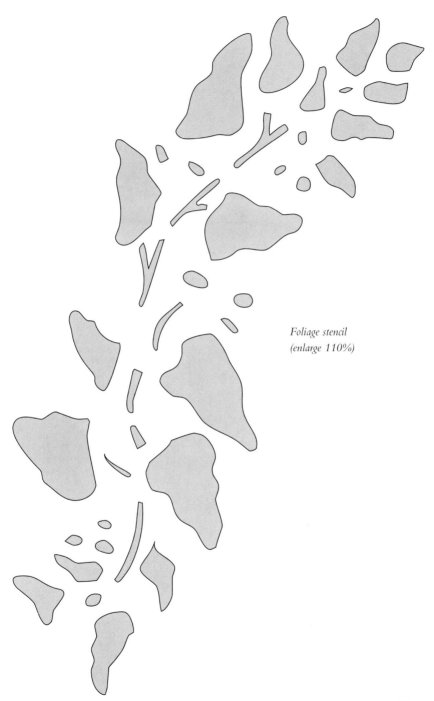

*Foliage stencil
(enlarge 110%)*

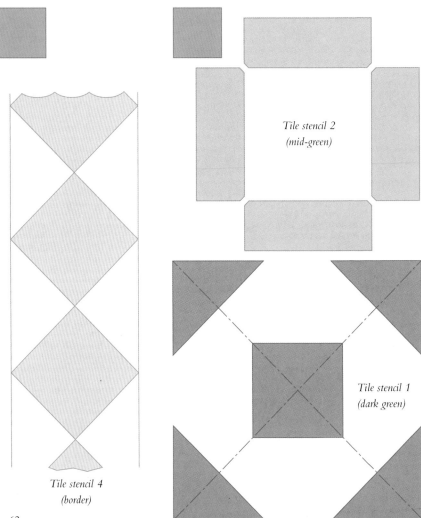

Tile stencil 3 (red)

*Tile stencil 2
(mid-green)*

*Tile stencil 1
(dark green)*

*Tile stencil 4
(border)*

Tools for decorating floors

Some of the most useful tools for decorating floors are shown below. Build up your tool kit gradually – most of the tools can be purchased from your local hardware or DIY store or craft outlet.

CLAW HAMMER *The round head is used to drive in nails, and the split claw pulls them out*

NAIL PUNCH *Used to punch nails below the level of the floorboards*

CRAFT KNIFE *Used for cutting stencils*

PAINT ROLLER *Frame with a replaceable sleeve; used to cover large areas with paint*

SMALL FOAM ROLLER *Used for applying paint to stencils*

FITCH BRUSH *Small stiff brush used for delicate tasks*

FILLER KNIFE *Used to apply wood filler when repairing floorboards*

FLAT BRUSH *Available in 50 mm, 75 mm and 100 mm sizes for general paint work*

UPRIGHT SANDER *Used to sand floors over a large area such as a room; can be hired when needed*

HAND SANDER *Electric sander used for small areas such as corners or awkward areas*

CORK SANDING BLOCK *Block around which abrasive paper is wrapped for sanding small areas and tight corners*

Index